Blog Post Ideas:

21 Proven Ways to Create
Compelling Content and Kiss
Writer's Block Goodbye

Danny Iny
Jim Hopkinson
Alexis Rodrigo

Questions

Questions can be sent to support@mirasee.com.

Dedicated to the bloggers who keep pounding their keyboards and hitting publish, even when it feels like nobody's paying attention.

Blog Post Ideas Extras

Free PDF Cheat Sheet + Blogging Expert Interviews + Online Video Companion Course

Get a one-page summary of the 21 blog post ideas, access to interviews of blogging experts, and a discounted price to the companion course!

Free PDF Cheat Sheet
Always have 21 blog post ideas within easy reach with this colorful cheat sheet.

Blogging Expert Interviews
Successful bloggers reveal how they bust through writer's block.

Online Video Companion Course – 50% off coupon
Enrich your discovery of the blog post ideas in this book. The video-based companion course is a different experience.

- 60+ minutes of video instructions
- Entertaining and educational
- Video walk-throughs of sample posts
- Bonus interviews of bloggers who've become published authors

Get your free cheat sheet, bonus interviews, and course coupon:

http://mrse.co/blog-ideas-extras

Website Links and Further Reading Available Online

Since this is a book about blog posts,
it refers to many blog posts.

To make your reading experience smoother, all links to
websites and blog posts mentioned in the book are
organized by chapter, in order of appearance, on this page:

http://www.mrse.co/blog-ideas-links

Happy reading!

Contents

INTRODUCTION
Welcome

"I'm sitting in my office trying to squeeze a story from my head. It is that kind of morning when you feel like melting the typewriter into a bar of steel and clubbing yourself to death with it" - Richard Matheson

It's every blogger's nightmare.

You fire up your word processor to write your next great blog post... and your mind is a blank.

You search the deepest corners of your brain... but the well of inspiration has dried up.

Your blogging deadline is looming... but your writing chops have disappeared.

Have you run out of things to say?

Is it time to quit your blog?

Relax, it's just writer's block. Every blogger goes

through it. Just look at the thousands of blogs that are abandoned or neglected, without any fresh posts for six months straight or more.

But since you're reading this book, we know you'll get through this. Your mind will fire up again. The well will fill again. And you will write good, even great, posts again.

We wrote this book for our fellow bloggers, content creators who know that your blog's success depends on your ability to churn out good posts... and to do it again and again.

Blogging is relentless. Not only do you need to continually deliver creative content your readers will love, but you also have to deliver great content week after week, month after month. You have to be both compelling and consistent. No excuses.

If you let writer's block, exhaustion, or creative ennui get to you, then your blog will fail. Your traffic will plummet. Your subscribers will forget you.

We've been there and we know how hard it is.

Who's "we"?

This book is based on the work of Mirasee's CEO, Danny Iny, the best-selling author of *Engagement from Scratch!*, *The Audience Revolution*, and *Teach and Grow Rich*. He started gaining prominence when he wrote 84 guest posts in 10 months. This feat also earned him the nickname, "Freddy Krueger of blogging," because he seemed to be everywhere all at once.

Mirasee's content crafter, Alexis "Lexi" Rodrigo, also contributed to the book. Her work has appeared on *Freelance Folder*, *Vero*, *Business2Community*, AWAI's *B2B Writing Success*, and *Copyblogger*, among others. For two years, she singlehandedly produced regular content for a software company's blog, YouTube channel, newsletter, and social media accounts.

Jim Hopkinson, Mirasee's Course Director, also co-authors this book. He has written more than 250 posts for his blog and 75 posts for *Salary.com*, and has been featured in *The Wall Street Journal*, *ESPN*, *WIRED.com*, *The Huffington Post*, *Men's Health*, *Success Magazine*, and many other sites.

Our company, Mirasee, works with small businesses and entrepreneurs like you who have a product, a service, or a message to share, and a genuine desire to help others with their unique voice. We provide in-depth training to help entrepreneurs build and scale profitable audience-based businesses.

We—Danny, Lexi, and Jim—have banded together to help you become an unstoppable blogger.

How to Use This Book

If you're reading this book before you actually need it, then you can read it straight through, from beginning to end. When you come across an idea you like, stop reading and go ahead and try it. This way, you'll find out which strategies work best for you even before writer's block pays you a visit.

But if you're reading this book in a moment of desperation, then read it like a cookbook. Skim through the "recipes" or ideas—there are 21 in all—and choose the one you can whip up most easily with the ingredients you have on hand.

We've included a speed rating to give you an idea of how quickly you can carry out each idea:

* One star means the idea takes a lot of planning, preparation, and/or time to implement.

** Two stars means the idea is easier, but still requires some time.

*** Three stars means the idea is super fast and will let you produce a new blog post in minutes.

We'll point you to plenty of real-life blog posts, so you can see each idea in action. You can also find them all listed on this page:

http://www.mrse.co/blog-ideas-links

You'll also meet two fictitious bloggers throughout this book: Fiona Food Blogger and Tommy Tech Blogger. They'll show you how the ideas can be implemented in diverse niches.

Finally, we end each idea with a Recipe for Success: the critical steps you must go through to carry out the tip.

To round out your experience of the book, we've created some **Blog Post Ideas Extras** for you.

There's a **free PDF Cheat Sheet**, which is a colorful summary of the 21 blog post ideas in the book. You'll want to print it out and hang it in your workplace for easy reference.

There are **video interviews** of successful bloggers, who share their own strategies to overcome writer's block.

And there's an **online video companion course** with over 60 minutes of entertaining instruction and walk-throughs of sample posts.

Get your access to these Blog Post Ideas Extras here:

http://mrse.co/blog-ideas-extras

"If you want to be a writer," Stephen King says, "you must do two things above all else: read a lot and write a lot." Reading this book is only half the work. To kiss writer's block goodbye and become the successful blogger you aspire to be, you need to actually execute the tips we share, and write.

Go now, read. And then write!

Capture the Magic

"Creativity is all around us, and some of the funniest, most beautiful, and touching moments happen when you least expect it." - Bryce Dallas Howard

For some people, the problem isn't *coming up* with ideas, it's coming up with ideas *at the exact point you need to write.*

Maybe you come up with great ideas *all day long*—in the shower, during your commute, on your lunch hour, during dinner with friends, right before you go to bed, in the middle of dreaming—but when you sit down to write that blog post a few days later, you have nothing. The idea has disappeared like the memory of a dream you're sure you had but now can't remember anymore.

If that's the case, you need a way to capture those ideas for later. Set yourself up for success by creating an environment where you can effortlessly record your thoughts and have them handy when you need them.

Our advice? Always be on the lookout for ideas!

Whether you're out shopping, chatting with friends, at the doctor's waiting area, or watching TV… ideas are everywhere!

Lexi, our content creator, got the idea for a 31-day series of blog posts while bored in a driving class. That series became the main lead magnet for a freelancing website.

You don't even have to wait for ideas to come. Turn yourself into what James Altucher calls an "idea machine." Sit down for a few minutes every day and force yourself to come up with at least 10 ideas for your blog. Some ideas will be good, most will probably be bad, but it doesn't matter. The point is to brainstorm 10 new ideas every day. That's how you strengthen your brain so it's always coming up with ideas.

How do you capture your ideas if and when they do pop up? You have many choices:

Notebooks and Journals

Let's start with the old-school method: pen and paper.

Don't dismiss this low-tech approach. Science shows writing by hand engages your brain's Reticular Activating System, or the filter that determines what you pay attention to and retain. No wonder writers like

Truman Capote and Susan Sontag preferred to write their drafts with a pen or pencil and paper.

Maybe Jim's old fashioned, but when he's attending a conference or sitting in a meeting, he feels it's impersonal to have a laptop out and be banging away on the keyboard while someone else is talking. That open laptop feels like a barrier. His format of choice is a medium-sized notebook that he throws in his backpack.

When some people hear "notebook," Moleskine is the first name they think of. Moleskines come in many sizes and varieties, lined or unlined. Lexi's favorite is the calendar Moleskine weekly notebook, because it lets her organize her week on half of the spread and jot down ideas on the other half.

When Jim's on the go, he downsizes to a smaller Moleskine journal, which is about the same size as his iPhone and fits right in his jeans or coat pocket. He even downsizes his pen, going from a Pilot G2 to a Pilot G2 mini.

Another great form of paper is the good old Post-It note. These sticky notepads are fun, because they're small, they're bright, and they're useful for capturing one specific idea at a time. You can place them near your desk or monitor, and move the ideas around to help organize your thoughts. Look at how our team used Post-Its to capture and organize ideas at our company retreat:

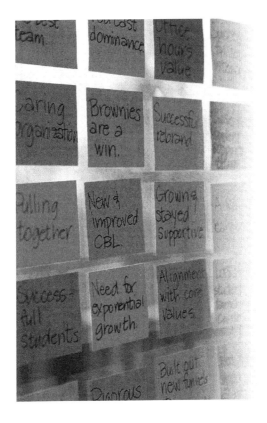

If you get your best ideas before you go to sleep, or even coming out of a dream, keep a pen and notepad next to your bed. As legend has it, the melody for the song, "Yesterday," came to Paul McCartney in a dream. As soon as he woke up, he ran to the piano and immediately played the song so he wouldn't forget it.

As much as Jim and Lexi love paper, it does have a drawback: you can't search in it for keywords!

Which is where the Mod notebook comes in. It looks like a normal notebook, until you get to the end and reach into its document pocket. You remove the pre-paid envelope, place the notebook in it, mail it to them, and they scan every page for you so that you have it digitally and can access it via the cloud. Now you can search your notes for any word or phrase and easily find it in the digital document.

Software and Electronics

For some of you, writing down notes on paper is as primitive as using a typewriter.

Everyone has their own system. If you're more comfortable on your desktop, laptop, or tablet, then set up documents and folders to record and organize your thoughts.

Better yet, store your information in the cloud using a service such as Google Drive or Dropbox, which allows you to access your notes at any time from any device.

Some people are fanatical about Evernote, just like our co-worker Charles Byrd, Director of Partnerships. He's an Evernote Certified Consultant and offers an online productivity course called Zero-to-60 with Evernote. He takes it to the next level, using Evernote to capture ideas and to record every important piece of business and personal information to streamline his life. From email and websites to handwritten notes and receipts, he can put his finger on anything he needs within 5 seconds.

And let's not forget that fast, portable, note-taking machine that's probably already in your pocket: your smartphone.

Here are six ways you can use your phone to capture ideas:

1) Keep it simple and record your thoughts on the notepad app that comes with your phone.

2) Download any of the apps for recording notes, thoughts, or to do lists.

3) Send yourself an email, which you can read and organize later.

4) See something interesting that sparks an idea? Take a photo. As a bonus, you can use the photo in your blog post later.

5) Better yet, record a quick video so that you remember what your idea was.

6) In your car or walking? Record a voice memo you can play back later.

A smartphone is a blogger's best friend.

Not Exactly Paper

And lastly, what if you get your best ideas in the shower? Don't let them go to waste! Aqua Notes is a product you can get for about $8, post up on the wall of your shower, and record your brilliant ideas before the shampoo runs into your eyes.

Whether you bubble with ideas all day long, sit down to brainstorm 10 ideas daily, or have just one good one per week, the key is to have a method to record ideas so they're at your fingertips when it's time to write.

Feel free to experiment with any and all of these options, or use them in combination until you find what works for you.

Choose the Best Tool for the Task

"Writer's Block: making authors miserable since the Stone Age." - Max Hawthorne

Now you've got ideas at your fingertips—great! You're ready to write.

But your creativity can get stifled if you have to wrangle with technology. The key is to find the easiest way to get your great idea and turn it into a blog post.

When it comes to writing software, you have many options:

Microsoft Word

Let's start with the good old standby, Microsoft Word. The program is now more than 30 years old, and some may find it slow, clunky, and bloated, but for writing blog posts, it's adequate. It tells you how many words and characters you've written. It even lets you track changes to your document, which is handy if you change your mind about something you deleted. So if you're used to it and it works for you, then stick with it.

The only downside is, if you copy and paste from Word to your blogging platform, it can copy a lot of the formatting code, messing up the way your post displays. When this happens, you'll have to strip away all that code before you publish your post.

Notepad/Text Edit

At the opposite end of the spectrum is a simple text editor. It's easy and fast, but doesn't have other bells and whistles. A lot of writers prefer this, because it's uncomplicated and doesn't inadvertently add any extra code like we just described.

Author George R. R. Martin, whose books were adapted into the show, *Game of Thrones*, revealed that he still uses WordStar, a DOS-based word processing program from the 80s. Seriously.

"I hate some of these modern systems where you type a lowercase letter and it becomes a capital," he says, "I don't want a capital. If I wanted a capital, I would have typed a capital. I know how to work a shift key."

Writing-Focused Programs

Frustrated with the gap between too complicated and too simple, new writer-centric programs have emerged that let you focus on one thing: writing.

One such option is Hemingway, a $10 app that a reported 2 million people used in its first year. Another is called BlankPage, which offers distraction-free writing and goal tracking.

You can find nearly 50 alternatives to Microsoft Word by using the site, AlternativeTo.net.

Google Docs

For many people, Google Docs is all they need. Google's word processor is robust, files are stored in the cloud, and it's easy to share with others when collaborating.

Scrivener

This book was written in a program called Scrivener. It's a $40 program that not only focuses on writing, but also lets you organize your thoughts, research, and other notes all in one document. It's packed with features for writers of books and scripts, but for bloggers, it's probably unnecessarily powerful.

WordPress

Lastly, for those who want to cut out the middleman completely, you can write your articles directly in WordPress.

The blogging platform allows you to save drafts, add formatting, and insert photos and videos, and it saves you the extra step of copying and pasting your post. Its distraction-free mode helps you to focus on writing, and leave the formatting for later. When you're done, either schedule your post for a future date, or simply hit publish.

If you're not happy with the writing program you've been using, explore these options. You'll be surprised how much more prolific you can be when you're using the correct writing tool.

Recipe for Success

- Use this book to become an unstoppable blogger: someone who publishes compelling blog posts consistently.
- Capture your ideas by keeping pen and paper, smartphone, or another tool handy.
- Choose writing software that lets you write efficiently with minimum distractions.

CHAPTER ONE
Cultivate a Prolific Mind

Creativity stems from the brain, and in this chapter, we will cover strategies to get your brain neurons firing with brilliant, new ideas.

Blog Post Idea 1: Get Creative through Organization *

"What you have to do is try not to force words to come.... Just make a list of all the things you want to say in any old order. Then later we'll figure out the right order." - Robert M. Pirsig

When most people think about creativity, they think about right-brained, far out, innovative ways to generate new thoughts to get you out of your comfort zone. We'll get to those soon.

In the meantime, let's look at how you can fuel creativity through what others may consider a very left-brained activity: organization. We're referring to your blog categories and an editorial calendar (a schedule of what posts you want to publish on specific dates).

When you take the time to plan a structure and schedule, you know the topics you're going to write about ahead of time. That takes a lot of the pressure off of you, and you gain the creative freedom to write *within* those constraints.

Blog Categories

It's helpful to you and your readers if your blog posts fall under specific "buckets" or main topics. Blog categories give an overall structure and guiding principle for your blog. When you need blog post ideas, use your blog categories as a starting point. For each category, ask, "what can I write about under this topic that would be helpful to my readers?"

Blog categories not only help you identify the specific topics to write about, but also help determine the audience you attract and, over the long term, how you rank for those topics in search engines.

But it extends beyond that, from the products you

launch to the guests you have on your blog and other content platforms.

Realizing the importance of blog categories, in early 2016, we brought the content team of Mirasee together to reorganize our blog categories. We streamlined them to the following:

1) Audience and Engagement

2) Courses and Education

2) Offer Creation

4) Business Reimagined

For example, this book is about attracting and growing your audience through blogging, so it falls under the Audience and Engagement category.

To identify your blog categories, consider mind mapping your topics on paper or using one of many available software options, such as XMind or Mind Meister.

Editorial Calendar

Once you've identified your blog categories, you can start to lay out an editorial calendar, slotting specific topics in advance so that when the time comes to publish a post, you can just look at what's coming up in your calendar, and write.

Of course, planning content in advance is easier for some niches than others.

Let's say you have a pop culture blog covering celebrities. It's impossible to plan a blog post about the Kardashians three months from now. Possibilities include a marriage, a divorce, a new TV show, a fashion line, a controversial tweet, or a polarizing magazine cover. Or maybe they won't be popular anymore next month. Who knows? Pretty much anything is on the table.

The same could be said if you run a finance blog covering the stock market. It's impossible to predict where things are going and what exactly you'll be writing about in two weeks.

This is where your blog categories can still provide a structure for your publishing calendar. For example, possible categories for a celebrity blog are fashion, relationships, awards, and movie/TV reviews. Posts for a stock market blog can be classified as either news, tips, or opinions. Even if the celebrity world and stock market change quickly, you can still plan your editorial calendar according to your blog categories.

You can also write evergreen content or topics that aren't time sensitive, such as "10 Surprisingly Useful Business Tips from the Kardashians" or "Are You Making These 7 Retirement Planning Mistakes?" to fill the gaps between content about current events.

Other niches offer more structure.

For example, while you won't know the outcomes in advance, if you write about politics, you know exactly when every election will be held. Or if you write about sports, you know exactly when every single game will be played. So even though we wrote this book in 2016, we can tell you that Super Bowl 52 will be held on February 4, 2018 at U.S. Bank Stadium in Minneapolis—and the stadium isn't even completed yet!

How do you fill in an editorial calendar? Here are the steps:

First, take a broad look at the entire year. Mark the major holidays like Thanksgiving and Christmas.

Also take note of holidays, celebrations, and events that are relevant to your niche. Fiona Food Blogger's editorial calendar, for example, shows celebrations like Pie Day, Hamburger Day, and National Men Make Dinner Day.

These special days make for compelling blog post ideas. Not to mention, posts around holidays and celebrations tend to get plenty of search engine traffic. Check out *Daysoftheyear.com* to find even the most obscure national days and celebrations.

Next, mark the days that are significant to you, like when you'll be on vacation—and not likely to be blogging—and when you plan to launch a new product, book, or special offer. If you know you're going to launch a new product in, say, mid-October, you can plan relevant posts leading up to your launch day.

You may also choose a theme for each month. Here are possible *monthly* themes for Tommy Tech Blogger's blog:

January – New Year, Consumer Electronics Show
February – Super Bowl TVs, Virtual Reality
March – SXSW conference
April – Spring electronics preview
May – Summer camera roundup
June – Dads and Grads
July – Business Breakthrough Conference
August – Back-to-school computers and gadgets
September – Apple iPhone announcement
October – Best tablets and eBook readers
November – Holiday electronics preview
December – Gadgets of the year

Notice how holidays and special events help shape the monthly themes on Tommy's blog?

Now drill down and sketch things out on a *weekly* level. Since Tommy Tech Blogger knows that the Consumer Electronics Show is in the third week of

January, he can plan his content around that, like this:

January, Week 1
 Year in Review/Best of Previous Year
 Consumer Electronics Show teasers
January, Week 2
 Flashback from previous year
 Bold predictions
 Consumer Electronics Show preview
January, Week 3
 "Live" from the show
 Video interviews
 Breaking news and trends
January, Week 4
 Consumer Electronics Show Highlights
 Hits and misses; winners and losers
 What this means moving forward

Let's say Fiona Food Blogger publishes a new post *daily*. She can have a theme for each day of the week, like this:

Monday: Meatless Mondays, vegetarian/vegan topic
Tuesday: New kitchen products, cookbooks
Wednesday: Wordless Wednesday (Single photo or photo essay)

Thursday: New recipe

Friday: Fan Friday (Answer a reader's question)

Saturday: Long form stories, step-by-step how-to's

Sunday: Beverages, wines

If Fiona were planning her posts for the Fourth of July week, it could look like this:

Monday: Meatless Fourth of July barbecue ideas

Tuesday: Cookbook review

Wednesday: Photo essay of traditional Fourth of July dishes through the years

Thursday: Recipe: Fireworks Cake

Friday: Fan Friday: "What are the best picnic dishes that don't go bad even when it's hot out?"

Saturday: How to Decorate A Star Spangled Banner Cake

Sunday: 7 Best Fourth of July Drinks

Do you see how this works? By deliberately setting your blog parameters in advance, you actually *help* your creativity, not constrain it. Structure helps unleash creativity.

Recipe for Success

- Choose 3-8 categories or main topics for your blog.
- Create an editorial calendar and fill in major holidays, special days, and events specific to your niche, important personal days, promotions, and monthly themes.
- Schedule specific post topics in your editorial calendar.

Blog Post Idea 2: Set Your Mind Free **

"All truly great thoughts are conceived by walking." - Friedrich Nietzsche

When you're facing writer's block, you're trying to get your mind to cooperate. That's why some call it "wracking your brain."

But the solution isn't to push your brain to work *harder;* it's the opposite: set your brain free to do what it wants to do.

An excellent way to do this is by going for a walk. You've probably heard this advice a hundred times before: Take a break, get up from your desk, go for a walk, and get some fresh air.

There's a lot of science and history behind the

benefits of walking for writers.

Famous walkers include Henry David Thoreau, Charles Dickens, CS Lewis, and Nassim Taleb. William Wordsworth might have walked as many as 180,000 miles in his lifetime, according to an article in *The New Yorker* called "Why Walking Helps Us Think."

The same article says that when we walk, more blood and oxygen circulate in our brains, and new connections between brain cells are created. More connections means better memory and improved thought processing.

This may explain why studies have found that walking helps improve creativity.

One Stanford study had students sit at a desk, walk on a treadmill, or saunter around campus. On one test, students came up with 4-6 times more creative ideas while walking—even on the treadmill. And on another test, 95% of the walking students came up with a creative metaphor, compared to only 50% of the ones who stayed sitting. How did the two Stanford researchers come up with the idea to run this study? On a walk, of course.

And walking in a garden may be better for your memory than walking on busy streets.

A study conducted at the University of South

Carolina showed that "students who ambled through an arboretum improved their performance on a memory test more than students who walked along city streets." Apparently, a busy city, with crowds, cars, and lots of distractions will zap your attention more than a casual stroll through a garden. So look for a quiet place to walk, where you'll be close to nature.

Another important factor is *how* you walk.

A *BBC News Magazine* article, "The slow death of purposeless walking," talks about the need for—and the slow death of—what is called purposeless walking. This isn't your daily commute to the subway or going from Point A at home to Point B at the corner store for a gallon of milk. Rather, it's an aimless stroll without a purpose. Some might call it wandering.

This means not listening to music, tuning into your favorite podcast, or having a fixed route while you walk. Too bad for Tommy Tech Blogger, but he shouldn't walk with his head down, buried in his smartphone, staring at Google Maps, reading email, or texting. For maximum benefit you shouldn't even walk with a friend.

It seems counter-intuitive that the best way to overcome writer's block is to stop trying to write, shut the computer, and go out for a walk. You may feel like you're slacking off. But it works. When you return to the computer, your mind will be fresh, you'll be in a positive mood, and the words will flow freely again.

But maybe the solution for you isn't taking a walk. We all have different triggers for our high-performance mental states. It's just a matter of finding the right triggers for you.

For example, Jim managed to have a streak where he wrote a blog post every Sunday night for five years— more than 250 posts in all.

Some weeks, he had an idea planned in advance, other weeks he interviewed a guest, and sometimes inspiration came to him easily. Were there many times when Sunday night rolled around and he didn't have a clue for a topic? You bet.

For Jim, the solution was simple. He's a huge runner and usually went for a long run every Sunday. He'd lace up his sneakers, leave his New York City apartment, and carefully navigate busy intersections, crowds of people, and a steady stream of frantic taxicabs.

Ten minutes later, he would be cruising along the East River path with other joggers. As the water flowed next to him, so did the ideas. And the longer he ran, the more inspiration he had. And not once—not once—did he return from a run without an idea for that week's blog post.

If you're looking for inspiration, get out of your

head and out for a walk. Or a run. Whatever works best for you.

Recipe for Success

- Take a break.
- Disconnect from music, podcasts, texts, and other inputs.
- Go for a leisurely walk or run, preferably close to nature.

Blog Post Idea 3: Change the Scenery **

"I've always said 'Writer's Block' is a myth. There is no such thing as writer's block, only writers trying to force something that isn't ready yet." - Julie Ann Dawson

For many writers, the key to creativity and prolific writing is having a set routine.

Stephen King talks about starting every single day with the same routine, beginning at the same time, sitting in the same seat, with his papers arranged in the same way, and writing 10 pages without fail. He has said, "It's not any different than a bedtime routine… Do you go to bed a different way every night?"

You can read more about the odd habits and curious

customs of famous writers on the site, *Brain Pickings*, if you're looking for a routine you can try.

But if your routine *isn't* working, you need to change things up. So while the previous section talked about getting out of your head and walking or running to spur new ideas, another way to stir the pot is to change the *location where you write*.

In today's day and age, that's become a lot easier. While it might have been quite a chore for Stephen King to lug a massive typewriter, paper, and manuscripts from place to place when he first started writing, today we have feather-light laptops and plentiful Wi-Fi.

This gives you a lot more mobility to find a new venue for inspiration and productivity.

You can begin by optimizing your current writing space. In an interview with Danny, Ron Friedman, author of *The Best Place to Work*, shared that productivity increases when our workspaces have natural light and indoor plants. These are things to consider as well when you're looking for a new location to work in.

For Lexi, moving to a new place to write simply means walking from her home office to the dining room. Or from inside the house to her front porch or garden. Sometimes that's enough of a change to reboot her brain.

On the other hand, when writing the companion Udemy course to this book, Jim combined a new venue and a new routine to optimize his writing and creativity. He got out of his apartment and over to his local coffee shop, where his server, Maggie, knew his preferred seat and preferred drink (a large latte), and he wrote free from the distractions of email.

If a coffee shop is still too distracting for you, check out the plethora of new co-working spaces opening up in cities around the world. Whereas your neighborhood Starbucks might not be ideal in terms of the consistency of their Wi-Fi and the danger of leaving your laptop unattended while you run to the bathroom, companies like WeWork are providing an office away from home for freelancers who crave that kind of structure.

And if you want to not only get out of the house, but also get outdoors, bring that laptop to the park or a restaurant that has an outdoor garden, patio, or roof deck. Fiona Food Blogger usually writes, appropriately, in her dining room. But for a creativity-boosting change of scenery, she could try writing in an outdoor cafe.

And finally, the ultimate destination is a writer's retreat. Some are fortunate enough to have a second home by the beach or a cabin in the mountains to escape to.

Can't you just picture yourself banging out post after post while sitting in front of a bay window as the waves roll in, or while curling up next to a fire in your rustic log cabin?

But for most of us, until we become internet rich and famous, we need to, well, get creative. With a small budget, a single weekend away at a hidden Airbnb can set the tone for a productive writing session to crank out a month's worth of blog posts.

So if you're looking for creative ideas, try looking outside your home or office.

While Stephen King fans might caution that this didn't work out so well for fictional characters like Jack Nicholson in *The Shining* or James Caan in *Misery*, in the real world, it's usually pretty effective.

Recipe for Success

- Optimize your workspace for productivity.
- Write in a different location, such as a coffee shop, restaurant, co-working space, cottage, or Airbnb.
- Change your routine until you get your writing groove back.

Blog Post Idea 4: Leave the Country *

"Traveling—it leaves you speechless, then turns you into a storyteller." - Ibn Battuta

Getting creative is all about getting out of your comfort zone, and there's no better way to do that than getting out of your country.

Now of course this is easier said than done, and might be impossible for those with young children or limited resources, so we'll give you an alternative in just a minute. But if you're able to pull it off, jumping on a plane to an exotic location opens up many creative paths.

In fact, let us show you how Jim was able to approach international travel in three different phases, and the resulting stories he got for his blog.

Phase 1: The "working" vacation

When Jim was working full-time at *WIRED.com* as a marketing director, he was also running his blog and podcast on the side. With about a year of planning, putting aside money, and saving up vacation days, he flew with two friends to Tokyo for two weeks. Jim believes that if you're a North American looking for a global location for inspiration and crazy cultural ideas all around you, Tokyo is the place to go.

While it would have been easy to write about the usual things… the delicious sushi at the Tsukiji Fish Market, the frenetic subway, the gorgeous shrines and temples of Kyoto, or the buzzing sidewalks of Shibuya… two unusual topics grabbed Jim's imagination.

The first was the incredibly high level of customer service, unlike anything he had experienced in the United States. This prompted a post, "Ritz-Carlton Service at a Red Roof Price–Why Japan Is King of Customer Service." Not only did this become a popular post for Jim's blog, but *WIRED.com* ran an excerpt and linked to his blog.

The second topic that fascinated Jim was, believe it or not, the toilets. If you've ever been to Japan or know about all the gadgets and buttons on their toilets, then you know what he's talking about. During Jim and his friends' exploration of the city, they somehow ended up at the Toto Toilet showroom, which he can only describe as a mix between IKEA, Home Depot, and the Apple Store.

Once again, it provided for a creative new topic for his blog, which he pitched to *WIRED.com*, and it's right up Tommy Tech Blogger's alley: "Wired-O-Nomics: What Japanese Toilets Taught Me About the U.S. Auto Industry."

Jim couldn't have experienced a new level of customer service without this international travel, and he *never* would have been able to write a story about crazy robotic toilets if he had been sitting at his desk at home.

Phase 2: The digital nomad

Another way to blog while traveling is as a digital nomad. When Jim started his own business, he had the freedom to work from anywhere. After reading about Buenos Aires in the book, *The 4-Hour Work Week*, it sounded like as good a place as any to spend a few weeks writing and working.

While there, Jim churned out a batch of blog posts and dripped them out over time when he returned home. Here are some ideas for how he did it, to serve as inspiration for you.

- First, he wrote an overarching post called, appropriately, "How to Work Remotely From Buenos Aires."
- Then he took the questions he had before going on the trip, and answered those questions through blog posts, based on his experience on the road and how his decisions turned out.

Here are the seven questions he started with and the posts that evolved from them:

1) Where am I going to stay? - "Review: Best Hotel in Buenos Aires"

2) How am I going to work there? - "Review: Urban Station Coworking Space"

3) What should I pack? - "Gadget Packing List for International Travel"

4) How will my new laptop perform on the road? - "Review: On the Road with the Macbook Air"

5) How will I make money while I'm there? - "How I Generated 9 Income Streams within 30 Days of Getting Laid Off"

6) How do I deal with international roaming charges? - "How to Set Your iPhone for international Travel"

7) What can I do for fun when I'm not working? - "Fun Things to Do in Buenos Aires while Working Remotely"

Surely these are the same types of questions other travelers have. Jim simply gave them the answers in an informative and entertaining way through his blog posts.

Phase 3: The travel blogger

The third phase is the travel blogger. Two years after the Argentina trip, Jim was itching for another international adventure, when friends invited him to their wedding in Singapore. It sounded like a great excuse to explore Southeast Asia. But flying halfway around the world isn't cheap, so he looked for ways to save on costs.

Jim had connected with a travel writer named Chris Alford at a conference, who ran the site *Love, Play, Work* with his wife Hannah, and they gave him tips on pitching hotels. Figuring he had nothing to lose, he reached out to hotels in Bangkok, Chiang Mai, and Krabi, Thailand, and asked them to sponsor his blog for a month. In return, he offered to write a few posts, mention the hotels on his podcast, take lots of photos and videos, and spread the word on social media. Long story short, one hotel gave him a free night, another gave him four free nights, and a third gave him two nights free and two nights at 50% off!

In Thailand, Jim followed the same formula he used in Buenos Aires to come up with fresh posts: a post on how to work remotely from Thailand, three different hotel reviews (with lots of photos and fun videos in three different cities), and another post about cool things to do in Thailand.

Jim wasn't even a travel blogger. He just wrote a few posts while on vacation, and the fresh cultural angle spiced up his blog.

Imagine all the exciting posts Fiona Food Blogger would come up with, if she were to go on a food trip to Asia, Europe, or Africa (assuming she isn't from any of those continents). After taking a vacation, Tommy Tech Blogger could write about useful gadgets for tourists, the best software for organizing all those travel photos, and a roundup of the best selfie sticks.

It may come as a surprise, but traveling can be conducive to writing. Traveling both takes you away from the usual distractions *and* gives you a change of scenery. For example, Danny takes advantage of business trips to get a lot of writing done, with the help of his laptop, noise-canceling headphones, a 17-inch external USB monitor, and a portable mouse. In fact, he wrote his book, *The Audience Revolution*, in a hotel room.

Unlike Danny, Lexi only needs an iPad with a keyboard when traveling. For her, the mere act of getting from one place to another is a writing opportunity. She has written blog posts in cars, airplanes, and airports. Her motto: "When all you can do is sit, you might as well write."

Finding culture at home

We're not suggesting you book an overseas trip every time you have writer's block. But even if you don't have the time or resources to fly halfway around the world, you can still use new cultural experiences to awaken your creativity.

Why not start with an authentic restaurant? Go somewhere you aren't familiar with, and pay close attention to the experience. It could be a Japanese sushi bar, an Argentinian steakhouse, or the Thai restaurant that just opened. In all likelihood, the food, decor, and music will be a cultural adventure for you. All the better if you can talk to the chef or a knowledgeable food server to learn about the back story of the food you're eating.

Other ways to expose yourself to new cultures include visiting a museum, watching a foreign play, or signing up for a class and learning a new language. Fiona Food Blogger only needs to walk down the international food aisle of her grocery store to get inspiration for new posts. Oh, the possibilities!

All this exotic experience is fodder for analogies and insights that can get your creative juices flowing. So whether you find culture around the world or around the block, think globally for your next idea.

Recipe for Success

- Expose yourself to new cultures by traveling to foreign countries.
- Take advantage of the solitude and new scenery to get plenty of writing done.
- Explore new cultures in restaurants, museums, stores—anywhere you can have a cultural experience—even in your own backyard.

CHAPTER TWO
Build on Other People's Content

Steve Jobs used to quote Pablo Picasso: "Good artists copy, great artists steal."

We're not telling you to steal or plagiarize, of course, but to "borrow with the author's blessing." Rather than turning inward to pull creative ideas from your own brain, look outward for inspiration and use what others have created as building blocks you can use for your blog.

Blog Post Idea 5: Ask the Audience **

"There are few experiences as depressing as that anxious barren state known as writer's block, where you sit staring

at your blank page like a cadaver, feeling your mind congeal, feeling your talent run down your leg and into your sock." - Anne Lamott

As a blogger, your job is to give your readers value by publishing the content they're clamoring for.

Sometimes you might *think* you know what your audience wants, but your posts miss the mark and get a lukewarm reception.

Sometimes writers are blind to their readers, thinking, "I'm just going to write whatever resonates with me, and my readers can take it or leave it." Not only is that incredibly selfish; it also guarantees you'll have fewer readers.

If you're looking for new blog post ideas that will lead to high traffic and higher engagement from your audience, why don't you try this radical idea: ASK THEM.

Here are five ways you can do this:

1) Ask for ideas in a blog post or email.

Publish a post or send an email to your subscribers and ask, "what would you like me to write about?" How you frame it will depend on your style, your connection with your audience, and your level of transparency.

If you're comfortable being brutally honest and transparent, go ahead and say, "Hey everyone, I'm flat out of blog post ideas and I need help. What should I write about this week?"

You may come off looking lame, though. After all, you're supposed to be a thought leader, and your readers look up to you. Admitting you're out of ideas might cause them to say, "Geesh, I thought this person knew what they were talking about." For this reason, we can't see a high-profile blogger like Seth Godin doing anything like this.

A more subtle way to frame it would be to add some explanation, give context around topics, make the reader feel more involved, and talk about it in terms of your editorial calendar (which we covered in Idea #1). This shows you've done the work and are validating your initial ideas.

For example, Fiona Food Blogger could write something like this:

Hey readers! I'd love your input.

I'm planning some great new content for the end of the year, and I only want to publish what's most helpful to you. So tell me: which of these topics would you like to read about before the holidays?

- *How-to articles for preparing major holiday meals like Thanksgiving turkey or Christmas ham?*

- *Creative ideas for side dishes?*
- *Fast-prep meals to get you through the busy holidays?*
- *Healthy menus to avoid holiday weight gain?*
- *Gift ideas for the chef in your life?*

If there's a particular topic I haven't covered that you'd like me to delve into, or a new idea you'd like me to explore, tell me about it, too!

Ideally, you'll get a mix of responses, giving you both insight into your audience and new inspiration. If the majority of people say they want fast-prep meals, then it's a sign that your readers are busy people who crave simpler recipes, because they don't have time to cook complicated meals.

By asking an open-ended question at the end, a fun, quirky idea may come up unexpectedly. Fiona Food Blogger may discover that her readers want to know more about spiralizers—a topic she never would have thought about.

Upon checking on Amazon, she discovers a spiralizer with more than 5,000 reviews, 200 questions, and appetite-stimulating photos of veggies, pasta, and onion rings. That leads her to discover spiralizer accessories, spiralizer cookbooks, and spiralizer alternatives. After seeing *5,000 people* taking the time to leave reviews and post photos of just one spiralizer, she realizes how a single topic could, well, *spiral* out of control and give tons of ideas.

2) Ask for ideas on social media.

Don't have a lot of readers or subscribers yet? Or don't want to put yourself out there with an entire blog post or email? Keep things short and sweet with a 140-character question on Twitter or a sentence or two on Facebook:

Hi! I'm sitting down this weekend to brainstorm new blog topics. How can I help you? What do you want to learn more about?

3) Ask for ideas through a survey.

If you have a large following who loves to give feedback, then a more efficient way to gather input is through a survey. Scanning through blog post comments or replies on Twitter can be time-consuming and messy, so another option is to make a simple, one-question survey with a free tool like Survey Monkey or Google Forms.

4) Ask for inputs on a problem.

Have your readers and contacts help you solve a dilemma.

For example, Tommy Tech Blogger likes working in a coffee shop, but he worries about leaving his laptop unattended whenever he goes to the bathroom. He's been using a notebook lock, but wonders if there's an even better solution. To find out, he publishes a post asking readers what they've been using and how it's been working out for them.

When Marcus Sheridan published a post asking the readers of his blog, The Sales Lion, to help him create a tagline for his site, the post received 143 comments.

This idea gives you a topic for your post and does a great job of engaging your readers as well.

5) Ask for input as soon as someone joins your tribe.

A great way to keep the ideas flowing on a regular basis is to ask your audience a question as soon as they sign up for your e-mail list. Set up your autoresponder to send a welcome email to each new subscriber.

Conclude the welcome email by saying something like, "Hit reply and tell me what is the one thing you're struggling with," or "Reply to this email and let me know a topic you'd like to hear more about."

If you're one of Mirasee's subscribers, you know that Danny's welcome email ends like this: "hit reply, introduce yourself, and tell us how you're hoping we'll be able to help you? :-)"

Many of the responses will be the same—and that's a good thing—as it shows you trends of what your audience wants. But you'll also get a random response here and there, which could make for great blog posts.

The easiest way to find out what your readers want is to ask them. So just ask, and you will receive.

Recipe for Success

- Decide where you want to ask your audience for ideas: your blog, email, or social media.
- Frame your question in a way that shows your desire to serve your audience.
- Ask, monitor replies, and collect blog post ideas.

Blog Post Idea 6: Use Your Friends **

"It is one of the blessings of old friends that you can afford to be stupid with them." - Ralph Waldo Emerson

If you're tapped out for ideas, one great way to spark new blog topics is to reach out to your friends and family.

Sometimes you only need to talk to a good friend to get a new perspective. It can actually be an advantage if said friend is NOT involved or even familiar with your niche.

So if you're running a parenting blog and feel like you've covered just about every parenting tip there is, talk to a friend who *doesn't* have children. They might bring up an interesting outside perspective as a non-parent, remind you that most people want to hear about the basics that you think have already been done to death, or maybe they're going through a completely different type of challenge that you can relate back to your blog.

Tommy Tech Blogger could talk to his friend, the middle-aged writer who's happily living his life without a smartphone and laptop, for example.

You can also mine your "online friends" for ideas. We're referring to people loosely associated with you on Twitter, Facebook, or other social sites. Since they don't know you personally, they often bring a different dynamic since they only know you from your online persona.

A third group to tap into are fellow bloggers or colleagues. If you work at a company and have a blog on the side, take a spin around the office and listen in on the water cooler conversation. Are people talking about the latest *Game of Thrones* spoilers? A viral video that you somehow haven't seen yet? Or a unique spin on the old clichés—weather, traffic, sports, and relationships?

A fourth source of inspiration are other like-minded entrepreneurs. Perhaps you're in a mastermind group, a professional organization, or a local, in-person meetup. You're probably already a member of a Facebook or LinkedIn Group for a topic related to your blog (and if not, why not?). Maybe you even pay for it. Get in there, ask a question, and turn the responses into blog post ideas.

And lastly, reach out to family members. After all, they probably know you best.

Just be prepared for your mom to tell you to write about the time you fell off the swings and broke your ankle at the playground when you were six. But, hey, she'll be glad you called.

Or perhaps your little brother will bring up the time you gave him horrible advice. Again. But combine the two and there's your post right there: "What a broken ankle taught me about giving advice to family members."

Finally, why not reach out to an elderly aunt or grandparent? With a lot more life experience to draw from, they can be a surprising source for stories.

Tommy Tech Blogger could ask gramps how he courted grandma before there was texting and Snapchat. Fiona Food Blogger could ask her nonna how she baked moist, fluffy cakes when electric mixers weren't invented yet.

Isn't it nice to know the people who are nearest and dearest to you can be involved in your blog? This is one of the few times when it's okay for you to use your friends.

Recipe for Success

- Ask friends, family, and social media connections for ideas around your topic.
- Listen in on conversations, both in real life and online, to find out what people are talking about right now.
- Learn something new from people, including those who aren't familiar with your niche.

*Blog Post Idea 7: Let Others Talk ***

"No one leaps up to say, 'Oh look, that paragraph was clearly written on an 'off' day.'" - Neil Gaiman

Interviewing is a great way to come up with content,

because the interviewee creates the content for you.

When Jim had a blog and podcast, he ran it as sort of a hybrid model. Sometimes, he was bursting full of ideas and couldn't wait to get them out on the web. He turned on the microphone or took to the keyboard and just ranted.

Other times, when he had met someone really interesting, he interviewed guests. A few times a year, he'd go to a conference with his podcasting gear, and record half a dozen interviews in just a few days, which he could then turn into blog posts.

Producing multiple stories in batches is one of the more popular tactics for overcoming writer's block and being efficient. You store up several posts so you're not scrambling for a new idea whenever it's time to publish a new post.

While Jim did his podcast interviews then turned them into blog posts, you don't have to go that route. You can conduct the interview by email. Or if you're more comfortable actually speaking to the person, you can do the interview on Skype and have the benefit of having a video for your YouTube channel, as well as a post for your blog.

Interviewing people is a win-win. Here's why.

Say you meet someone interesting at a conference, and they tell you about the new app, book, product, or course they're launching. Maybe Fiona Food Blogger meets someone who just wrote a book about a gluten-free diet. Or maybe Tommy Tech Blogger meets someone who's launching a new app. Fiona and Tommy just met people who could be perfect to interview on their blogs.

The interviewees are thrilled because they get to promote their product, and Fiona and Tommy are happy because they just got off the hook for coming up with an idea for another post, especially on topics they know their readers want to know about but where they don't have expertise.

You just have to be naturally curious, do some background research, and ask good questions. It's a lot easier to write a handful of interview questions than it is to write an entire post.

The other benefit of interviewing people on your blog is, they're likely to spread the word about your blog post to their audience. This means new readers for your blog!

And while it's gratifying to talk to a published author or someone famous, even someone internet famous, Jim found it just as satisfying talking to friends, vendors, other bloggers, and members of his audience.

There are two ways you can create a blog post through interviews. You can go deep with one interviewee in one blog post. For example, Lexi interviewed Skellie, author of *The Blog Business Funnel*, and produced a two-part post: "How to Find Clients with Your Blog (Even If You're Not a Freelance Writer)."

Or, you can ask several influencers or peers the same question and compile their answers in one guest post. Here's a post where marketer Nicole Dean asked this question: "What is your #1 tip for a great About page on your website?" She also included screenshots of her interviewees' About pages, which made for a visually appealing and informative post.

As you can see, a new post can be as simple letting someone else do the "talking."

Recipe for Success

- Be on the lookout for people who'd be interesting to interview on your blog.
- Do your research and prepare good interview questions. What would your readers ask?
- Write a brief but engaging introduction and a call to action for the end of the interview post.

Blog Post Idea 8: Welcome Guests *

"When the ink runs dry, you're most likely writing at the wrong angle." - Carolyn Shields

The only thing better than interviewing someone for your blog and having them provide *most* of the content, is having someone write a guest post for you and provide *all* of the content.

Soliciting guest posts is a great way to source content, and it's easier than most people think. First, find a handful of blogs the same size or smaller than yours, whose content you really like, and invite the blog owner to write a guest post for you. Danny calls this, "embracing the nobodies."

They'll be flattered, happy to get exposure to your audience, and work hard to provide their best work. Not only will you get a great post, but they'll also tell their contacts about it, and bring you a few new readers in the process.

If you're going to implement this strategy often and want to receive guest posts without approaching bloggers, put up a "Write for Us" page on your blog. Include writing guidelines, even a simple one, for your guest authors.

Your guidelines should cover:

- The type of content you're looking for
- Length of posts
- Number and types of links writers can include
- Format for the byline
- If you pay contributors
- Photo and image requirements
- What you expect the guest blogger to do in terms of responding to comments on their posts and promoting to their audience

While we encourage you to use this strategy *purposely*, the first guest post on Jim's blog happened by accident. *Literally*.

He had been religiously writing posts each and every week, until a birthday mountain bike trip left him with an unexpected present: a broken arm. Jim's marketing assistant, Brandon, offered to take over the blog while Jim was out, and proposed an interesting story.

A millennial in his early 20s, Brandon was constantly debating with his parents over technology. They were always on his case about how often he was using his cellphone, and they didn't understand how he could watch Netflix on his laptop and look at Twitter on his phone all at the same time.

Brandon thought, "They just don't get it." Then the idea came to him. This is how *his* parents must have felt when talking to *their* parents about rock and roll. From there the title hit him, "Social Media Is the New Rock and Roll," and he was off to the races with a masterfully crafted post.

Don't accept blog posts if they require major revisions. Draft guest posts should only need minimal edits and a brief introductory paragraph from you. Also run the draft through one of the many free online plagiarism checkers. You only want to publish 100% original guest posts.

And no matter how desperate you are for posts, always vet guest bloggers before giving them exposure on your blog. As Danny says, your blog is your house, and you decide who to invite as your guest and place in front of your readers.

Is it ok to let someone you trust take over your blog for a few posts? Just say, be my guest!

Recipe for Success

- Invite other bloggers to write a guest post for you.
- Put up a "Write for Us" page with writing guidelines for your blog.
- Do your due diligence and be selective about who you allow to guest post on your blog.

- Write an introduction for the guest post, to encourage your visitors to read it.

Blog Post Idea 9: Become a Curator **

"Creativity is knowing how to hide your sources." - C.E.M. Joad

The final way to borrow content from others is to curate existing content and publish it in a useful way. This is often called a "roundup post."

Here's the simplest way to make a roundup post:

Step 1: Make a list of your 10 favorite websites in your niche.

Step 2: Go to each of them and choose your absolute favorite post.

Step 3: Publish a post listing these top 10 posts, and explain why you like them.

That's it. You barely even have to think about being creative, because the creativity comes from the awesome articles you've selected.

The only work you need to do is to write an intro, add your own commentary or insight for each post, and craft a conclusion. Don't make your post merely a list of other posts or content; you'll look lazy. Instead, give your take on each piece of content you've included, which could be 1-3 sentences.

Another benefit of the roundup post is that the blogs you feature will appreciate you giving them a shoutout and driving traffic to their site. So much so that they're likely to tell their subscribers and social media followers about your roundup post!

You can keep using this idea by creating focused roundup posts around specific topics.

Want a real-life example? "July's Best of the Web—Business Blueprints and Templates" is, you guessed it, a roundup of the best sources of business blueprints and templates we've found on the web. The author didn't just list the sources willy-nilly, but organized them into sub-sections and wrote a short description of each.

Let's look at how this would work for Tommy Tech Blogger. Here are examples of ways he could curate content around the tech niche.

Problems and Products

Let's say Tommy Tech Blogger realizes he's gained 10 pounds, because he spends too much time sitting in front of his computer. He knows it might be a problem his readers have as well, so he decides to explore how technology can be used as a way to help with weight loss. So a sample roundup post on his blog could be "12 Best

Apps to Help You Cut Down on Calories," or "10 Ways to Lose Weight With the Help of Your Smartphone."

Another way to curate content is around products. Tommy Tech Blogger could write a post on "7 Upcoming Wearable Devices That Will Soon Become A Part of Your Daily Life," or "My Picks for the Top Online Coding Courses of All Time." And if you're an affiliate for these products, these posts could bring a nice chunk of change from affiliate commissions.

People

The next approach is to highlight the people in your industry. Possible headlines include "7 Tech Bloggers You'll Actually Learn From," or "Meet the Owners of the Most Promising Startups in Silicon Valley."

Social

Expanding on the people in your industry, you can direct readers to their social media accounts on Twitter, Instagram, Pinterest, Snapchat, or whatever the app du jour is. For example, "22 Tech Geeks You Need to Follow on Instagram," or "The 10 Most Interesting Developers to Follow on Twitter." When Elena Verlee published "20 Men Entrepreneurs to Follow on

Twitter" on *PRinYourPajamas.com*, it got so much traffic that her site crashed—a happy problem to have.

Resources

Think about resources as a master list of things your reader needs to accomplish a goal. For example, "Everything You Need to Start a Freelance Web Development Business" could point people to resources such as certifications, training, website development, business strategy, marketing materials, and so forth.

Media

Beyond bloggers or products, think about other forms of media you can curate, such as Slideshares, TED talks, YouTube videos, movies, or courses. Articles could include, "5 TED Talks That Will Change The Way You View Technology" or "The Ultimate YouTube Playlist If You Want to Understand Quantum Computing." As a bonus, blog posts with media like slides or videos embedded in them tend to rank higher in the search engines than plain text posts.

By gathering the best content on the web, you deliver valuable content to your readers without creating it from scratch.

Recipe for Success

- Decide on a topic for your roundup post.
- Look for the best posts or other media on that topic.
- Write an intro, summary or description of each item on your post, and a conclusion.

CHAPTER THREE
Launch from the Media

Remember back in the chapter, "Cultivate a Prolific Mind," when we urged you to get outside, have a change of scenery, get out of your head, and look for inspiration all around you?

You can also find inspiration in mass media content that bombards you every day. Keep your eyes open for it.

Blog Post Idea 10: Mine the Mass Media **

"Do you know we are ruled by t.v." - Jim Morrison

While being lazy, flopping on your couch, and binging on Netflix sounds like the *opposite* of what you should be doing when you have a blog post due, sometimes it's just the thing you need to spark a fresh idea.

Media professionals do this all the time. Have you noticed how news commentators talk about something they read in the newspaper? Or how content from websites—even YouTube—end up as fodder for TV shows? Media professionals cross-pollinate ideas from each other, and you can do the same.

Books

Let's start with the "anti-media": sitting quietly and reading a book. As the saying goes, "Write even when you don't feel like it. And when you can't write, read!"

Reading books can have many benefits to your writing, including producing new ideas, learning storytelling techniques, and improving your grammar and vocabulary.

You probably have books on your bookshelf that you've been meaning to read but haven't gotten around to yet. Now's the time to do it. Sit with a nice warm cup of tea or a glass of wine, and read. Mine the book for ideas you want to share with your blog readers. Even if you disagree with the author or hate the book!

Or go back to one of your favorite books and read it again. What keeps you coming back? You could blog about that.

Magazines

There's a magazine for every topic under the sun. If you head to the magazine rack at a major bookstore, you'll be surprised at how even the most obscure topics have a magazine dedicated to it.

Imagine Fiona Food Blogger doing this. With dozens of magazines about food and cooking, Fiona's problem is picking which magazine to look at first. Finally, she chooses *Clean Eating*, specifically the Quick & Easy issue.

"What's clean eating?" Fiona wonders. Hmm… maybe her readers want to know as well. She writes that down as a possible blog post topic. Then she reads the letters to the editor: did anyone point out something that was missed in a previous article? Or sing praises about a particularly helpful one? Two more possible topics for her blog.

Next, she flips through the articles: which ones could she put her own spin on? If quick and easy recipes are in demand, maybe she can do a month of quick and easy recipes on her blog.

She also takes note of the ads. Which products would be interesting for her to write about? Which company seems to be coming out with the most imaginative products? Could she interview someone from the company? By the time Fiona puts the magazine down, she has at least five new blog post ideas.

Radio and Podcasts

As you're going for that run, walking the dog, driving in your car, or even doing chores around the house, tune in to your favorite radio show or download a popular podcast. Listen for something that sparks a debate or an aha! in your mind, and turn it into your next post.

Movies

Block off a few hours to take in a movie. Don't just passively *watch* the movie, *study* it. From superhero movies with lots of explosions to compelling dramas or dialogue-driven films by Aaron Sorkin or Quentin Tarantino, picture yourself as the actor, the writer, or the director. Tommy Tech Blogger could binge on old Star Trek movies and write "21 Gadgets We Use Today That First Came Out In Star Trek."

And since sometimes truth is stranger than fiction, a documentary about your niche can be a rich source of blog post ideas as well.

Plays

If you think it's lazy to sit in front of your TV for hours on end, then watch a live theater performance with an engaged audience. It can stimulate your senses in a way no TV show can.

The theater is an abundant source of ideas, because there's so much more atmosphere, and so much more happening—and you're experiencing it all in real life! This means there's that much more for you to deconstruct and draw analogies from. Find a show in your area, get out of the house, and come back refreshed and ready to start writing.

Comic Books

Yes, even comic books can be a source of ideas for your blog. Nate Cooper, an entrepreneur, teacher, and writer who has contributed to sites like *Mashable.com*, turned his love of technology and comics into a book called *Build Your Own Website: A Comic Guide to HTML, CSS and WordPress*. While this is right up Tommy Tech Blogger's alley, a comic book doesn't have to be about your niche for it to be a source of inspiration for a blog post. Or several.

Television

And finally, there's good old television. According to Nielsen, the average American spends more than five hours a day watching TV, so if you're doing that instead of working on your blog, try to at least get some writing ideas while you're at it.

- Check out *CNN* or the nightly news to see what's happening in terms of world or local events. Watch out for current events that could affect your niche, or implicate your readers. For example, Fiona Food Blogger should be on top of food recalls and news about food poisoning, while Tommy Tech Blogger should be on the lookout for new gadgets on the market.

- Indulge in a Netflix binge of the hot new series. What story elements can you draw from? How do they hook the viewer at the very end of an episode and get them to say, "Ok, I swear, just one more episode and then I'm going to bed."

- Whether you view them as a guilty pleasure or a waste of time, dip a toe into the reality TV waters. Flip through a few episodes of *Real Housewives, The Bachelor, America's Next Top Model*, or a celebrity chef show.

- Tune into a live sporting event to see how real drama comes into play. What words do the announcers use to describe the action? What can you learn from passionate fans who act as if *they're* the ones playing the game? Can you translate a classic David vs. Goliath underdog battle into a story for your blog?

Here's a real-life example of how you can put this idea into action.

Jim saw comedian Louis CK on the Conan O'Brien show doing a hysterical bit called "Everything Is Amazing and Nobody Is Happy." He talked about how he was on a plane and the passenger next to him got angry when the new, high-speed, in-flight Wi-Fi broke down. CK grew angry. He felt we should all be constantly amazed at the miracle of flight, noting, "You're sitting in a chair, in the sky!"

This inspired Jim to write a post about the economics of traveling, which was perfect for his blog since it mixed business and pop culture. His post? "Business Class at 30,000 Feet."

Next time you'd rather watch TV or flip through a magazine instead of writing a blog post, go ahead and indulge. It just may be what you need to get a brand new idea for your blog.

Recipe for Success

- Pick a medium to mine ideas from: a book, magazine, TV, movie, theater… even a comic book.
- Stay on top of current events and other news in your niche.
- Don't worry about covering a similar topic on your blog that's been tackled in a different medium. Put your own spin on it.

Blog Post Idea 11: Make a Media Mashup **

"Mystery is at the heart of creativity. That, and surprise."
- Julia Cameron

You've taken a break from your computer and consumed a ton of media to generate ideas. What else could you do with that? You could combine lessons learned from media with your own knowledge to come up with a unique blog post.

The idea is to take two unrelated things, and force them together into a really interesting post. You're creating a mashup of two unconnected ideas—which makes your post original and interesting. Don't worry, it's easier than it sounds.

Start by picking something your readers are familiar

with, such as a type of music, and then relate it with a topic within your niche.

Copyblogger is particularly good at this approach. Some of their most popular posts are "5 Things Depeche Mode Can Teach You About Effective Online Marketing," "The Grateful Dead 4-Step Guide to the Magical Influence of Content Marketing," and "The Eminem Guide to Becoming a Writing and Marketing Machine."

You can create mashups with all forms of media:

Movies

Movies are a great way to make this connection, since you have a many options. You can use either the name of a movie, or a character from that movie, and because they're one of those things that stay with people for a long time, you have a lot of leeway in terms of genre. Here are three examples:

1) Nostalgia

Even though *The Princess Bride* came out in 1987, it's considered a cult classic for both young and old. *Copyblogger*'s Brian Clark referenced this in his post, "Inigo Montoya's Guide to 27 Commonly Misused Words."

If you know who that character is, chances are you're

going to click through and read the article. That it has more than 8,000 shares is a good sign that many readers recognized Inigo Montoya. But even those who didn't may have read it out of curiosity.

2) The breakthrough hit

Another way to capitalize on this technique is to latch onto the breakthrough hit. For example, Jim was working at *WIRED.com* when the movie, *Slumdog Millionaire*, came out. It had a suspenseful plot, great direction, an awesome soundtrack, and went on to win eight Academy Awards, including Best Picture.

Capitalizing on the excitement, Jim put together a post called "Marketing Lessons From *Slumdog Millionaire*," which *WIRED.com* ran a few weeks before the *Oscars*.

3) The blockbuster series

Sometimes a movie becomes so popular it remains in the public eye for some time. From *The Fast and the Furious* to just about every comic book adaptation ever made, leave it to Hollywood to seize one successful movie and then throw sequel after sequel after sequel at us. Sadly, this often works.

For example, did you know that a *Hunger Games* movie finished in the top 10 box office in 2012, 2013, 2014, and 2015, with a worldwide gross of nearly $3 billion dollars? The movie franchise got so much traction, even the big boys jumped on this topic for a story, showing up on the websites of *Forbes, Time, PR Daily, Inc.com*, and *Scholastic*. Even *Vogue* jumped on the bandwagon with a beauty and fitness contest.

Television

Same idea, but this time pick a television show your audience is probably watching. That's what Jon Morrow did in his hit post, "Mad Men Guide to Changing the World with Words," and Danny with "Desperate Housewives on Writing, Storytelling and Selling."

But you could also use a less popular show, as long as you can get your point across even to readers who aren't familiar with it. An example is Lexi's post, "Online Marketing Success Lessons from *The Next Great Baker*."

For extra credit, list the top five TV shows you can think of, and then do keyword research to see which one is most popular.

Books

You can also mashup a concept with a book from outside your blog's niche. For example, "What *How To*

Win Friends and Influence People Can Teach You About Winning Friends and Influencing People" would be lame.

The idea is to mashup two unrelated ideas to come up with something unexpected, remember? It doesn't even have to be a book; it can be an author, such as "What Stephen King Can Teach You About Fear and Courage," or, for Fiona's food blog, "12 Dinner Party Menus Inspired by Danielle Steel's Novels."

Comics

There's a reason why Hollywood's been remaking movies about Superman, Spiderman, the X-Men, and half a dozen other, more obscure comic book characters. Unless it's a spectacular failure, you can pretty much count on a certain volume of sales at the box office. By the same token, if you lean on the super-powers of one of these characters, your post should perform as well.

A word of caution: don't mash two ideas together unless you see a clear connection between them. Don't force what isn't there. Otherwise, your post will sound contrived.

Recipe for Success

- List popular media you're familiar with.
- Reflect on an episode, story, or character, and extract ideas, lessons, and other nuggets you can apply to a topic in your niche.
- Write your mashup post, making sure the analogies you draw are clear and logical.

Blog Post Idea 12: Please the Crowds ***

"Creativity is the process of having original ideas that have value. It is a process; it's not random." - Ken Robinson

If you want to give readers what they want, it's only logical to write posts about topics they're already interested in. Aside from asking them directly, as you learned in Chapter Two, you can take a cue from what they're already talking about, looking for, and sharing online and in real life.

Experts call this "newsjacking" or riding piggyback on already popular stories to make your own content appealing.

There are many ways for you to discover which topics are currently trending, such as:

Google Trends

Find out what web users worldwide are typing into Google by going to google.com/trends. Let the world's largest search engine show you the top stories trending now, a graph of search interest over time, the number of articles being produced around that topic, the region where the searches are taking place, and other related topics.

Twitter

Twitter is another great place to see what's current. Go to your Twitter homepage to check what's trending in your area or nationwide, scroll through Twitter Moments, or search for hashtags related to your niche.

Facebook

Take a quick scroll through your Facebook feed. You're likely to see the latest popular thoughts on politics or sports or simply people posting photos of their kids (which could be a topic right there). You might also spot a trend everyone's talking about—like the ice bucket challenge, if you were scrolling in July 2014—that seemingly comes out of nowhere, goes insanely viral for two months, and then dramatically fades away.

So grab it while it's hot.

Facebook also tells you what's trending through a little Trending box on the right-most column of its desktop interface. You can toggle from Top Trends to Politics, Science and Technology, Sports, and Entertainment. Since Facebook knows what topics you post about and engage with on the platform, it will show you the trends that are relevant to you.

Websites

Go to just about any popular website, from *Buzzfeed* to the *NY Times* to *CNN*, and look for the most popular and most shared articles to see what's hot right now. Simply take a topic and put your own spin on it.

Celebrities

And lastly, it seems celebrities change their thoughts and their styles by the week, so see what's new and interesting. No matter what your topic, you can usually find a celebrity angle. Let's take Tommy Tech Blogger, for example. Here are some celebrity-related stories he could write:

- Celebrities who invest in startups, such as Ashton Kutcher's various investments in tech startups (reportedly over 50 of them!) and Justin Bieber leading a $1.1 million seed round for Shots, a selfie sharing app.

- Android versus iOS at the Oscars: which mobile platform is more popular among celebrities?
- Or go anti-tech and write about celebrities who hate technology (they do exist!).

A "celebrity" doesn't have to be a famous movie star, athlete, or musician. You can use the term as a blanket category for any icon or influencer your audience would recognize, from a popular blogger to a YouTube star, to a successful entrepreneur.

Let's finish things up with an example.

By now, the average person probably knows the name, Elon Musk, the entrepreneur and CEO of electric car company Tesla. The progress, awareness, and interest around electric vehicles continues to grow at a rapid pace, and he appears in the news and on magazine covers more and more often.

But since Jim was previously working for a tech company and was covering this type of content in his blog, he had heard of Musk a few years before the general public did.

Using Google Trends, you'll see there wasn't much

search volume back in April 2013—a relative score of 13 out of 100—whereas in April 2016, he peaked at 100 out of 100.

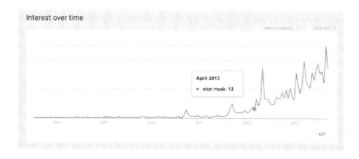

So if you were a new reader of Jim's blog and stumbled across his post, "Why Elon Musk Should Make You Feel Like a Loser that Has Never Accomplished Anything," you would feel like an insider since you would have been one of the first people to know about Musk.

It's fun to jump on a hot story and talk about the latest rising star. But even more importantly, you'll make your readers feel up-to-date and help them discover an emerging trend.

Recipe for Success

- Dig into Google Trends, Twitter, and Facebook to discover popular topics.

- Look for a celebrity angle within your niche.
- Keep an eye out for people who are on the cusp of fame and influence, or are already celebrities in their own right within your niche.

Blog Post Idea 13: Disrupt with Media *

"Think of it: a photographer presses a button. A few hours later and half a world away, some dots of ink on a news print showed what he had seen—and had the power to touch people's emotions, perhaps to change their way of thinking." - Soheir Khashoggi

Do you only ever put words to the page with an occasional photo? If so, it might be time to disrupt things.

Instead of focusing completely on your writing, mix it up by adding a new form of media to your post, like:

Photos

You might already be adding a photo or two to your posts, but are they truly *great* photos, or cheesy clip art or stock images? Only use great photos, for a change. Get away from your laptop, grab your phone—or better yet, that expensive DSLR that's been gathering dust on your shelf—and take some new and interesting pictures and make them the focus of your post, not just the supporting cast. Blog photos are especially important to get more traffic through Pinterest and Instagram.

Then go beyond just adding a photo to your page. Why not try a photo essay so that 80% of your content is photos and 20% is text, instead of the other way around. For inspiration, check out "The Big Picture," a fantastic photo blog on *BostonGlobe.com*, and see how even the most ordinary objects, events, and people can be captured in powerful photographs.

Lexi used photos to drive home her point in the post, "Proof: Bokashi Compost Grows Better Plants." The pictures clearly showed the difference in size and vigor of tomato plants grown in varying amounts of Bokashi compost. The post simply wouldn't have been as convincing without the images.

(Remember, all links to websites and blog posts mentioned in the book are available here: http://www.mrse.co/blog-ideas-links)

Photos definitely liven up a story. That's how Jim used photos from a business trip to make a blog post more compelling. After a conference, he was at a club with friends, when commotion and fanfare broke out. Employees streamed in to loud music, and six of them stood up holding giant cards that spelled out the name, REGGIE. Jim and his friends thought a famous Reggie must be in the club, but, no. It turned out to be *some ordinary guy named Reggie*, who paid extra for this service.

This led to a discussion about the "Look at Me Generation," and eventually an in-depth blog post entitled "Is This the Me Generation, or Has Social Media Just Made It That Way?" Sure, Jim could have written the post without photos, but they gave it more authenticity and personality.

Screenshots

Another kind of visual to liven up your posts is screenshots. People love to see how you do things, so if you're documenting something like how to code a website or the way you arrange your desktop icons for peak efficiency, screenshots are perfect to walk people through your process. You can take screenshots by using programs like Jing, Snagit, Camtasia, and Screenflow.

Tweets

See a great quote on Twitter? Use their embed feature to make it the focus of a post. You can either take a single tweet, analyze it, or use it as a jumping off point for a story.

Or combine multiple tweets from multiple sources to tell a story of an event, such as breaking news, a business announcement, the new iPhone release, a political misstep, or a controversial sports moment.

Infographic

Want to deep dive into a topic without writing a long, tedious post? Try an infographic. That's what we did at Mirasee to share the findings of our industry survey on online courses in the post, "The State of Online Courses [INFOGRAPHIC]." You can find more inspiration for infographics from the site, *CoolInfographics.com*.

You can make your own infographics using free and paid tools like Infogr.am, Piktochart, Easel.ly, Visual.ly, or Canva.

Or hire a designer to create one for you. Sites like *Fiverr*, *Upwork*, or *99designs* offer design services at reasonable fees.

Videos

No doubt, video consumption across every platform continues to rise. One video can transform the impact of your blog posts, and even take the place of hundreds of written words. However, even if you embed a video on your blog, your post should still have some text, for search engine optimization purposes.

For example, if Tommy Tech Blogger wanted to show how to upgrade the memory of his laptop, the best way would be to make a demonstration video. That would be clearer than a plain text explanation, even if accompanied by screenshots.

You don't need an expensive video camera, microphone, lights, and background screens to create good online videos. Your smartphone camera is probably good enough, as long as you're in a well-lit area.

If you are using your smartphone to record videos, remember to shoot with your phone in the horizontal position. This is because our eyes see horizontal images, which is why movie and TV screens are horizontal as well. Vertical videos are hideous to watch and make you look like an amateur.

We recommend the following tools for taking better videos with your smartphone:

- An external lapel microphone, such as the Audio-Technica ATR-3350, Rode Smartlav Lavalier, or Edutige EIM-001 iMicrophone
- A stabilizer, such as a monopod (aka "selfie stick"), tripod, or the Swivl

Got a crappy smartphone? Use the webcam and built-in microphone of your computer.

Another thing to remember when using video is that it's *critical* to have good audio. In fact, good audio is more important than having a crystal-clear image. Ironic, but true. Try watching a movie with a grainy image. As long as the sound is good, you'll still understand what's going on. Now try watching a clear video but with garbled or no sound. You'll soon get lost and confused.

So if you'll be creating lots of videos, a quality microphone is a good investment. Buy the best you can afford.

Here are different ways you can incorporate videos on your blog:

- Record your feelings on a topic. The next time you have a good rant, let it fly.

- Use video to demonstrate a specific procedure in a how-to post.
- Sit down with someone interesting and ask them some questions on camera.
- Try a live video like Periscope or Facebook Live and use that to spark conversation on your blog.
- Embed a quick video from Instagram.
- Make a story on Snapchat, export it, and embed it on your blog as a video.
- Embed TED Talks or somebody else's video from YouTube.

Recipe for Success

- Use visuals (such as photos, screenshots, infographics) or video so you can show *and* tell.
- When shooting a video with your smartphone, hold the phone horizontally.
- Make sure the audio of your video is crystal clear.

CHAPTER FOUR
Find the Good, the Bad, and the Ugly

You've probably experienced analysis paralysis: overanalyzing something so much, that you're paralyzed and can't make a decision. When blogging, every alternative looks like it could be something you *could* write about, and yet no single idea stands out as a *great* idea.

Put your analytical mind to good use. Blog about a case study, prediction, review, or how-to article. We'll explore those options in this chapter.

Blog Post Idea 14: Highlight the Good ***

"Convince yourself that you are working in clay, not marble, on paper not eternal bronze: Let that first sentence be as stupid as it wishes." - Jacques Barzun

Think about a website, blogger, or company you hold in high esteem. Maybe a podcast you can't wait to download every single week, a blogger who inspires you more than any other, or a company that always seems to do the right thing.

Once you have one in mind, do a case study analyzing why it's the best of the best and identifying lessons others can learn from your subject. The lessons make the post relevant and useful to your readers. Otherwise, you'd just be gushing without purpose.

Websites, Blogs, and Social Media

Start with your favorite websites and blogs. Which ones do you find yourself reading day after day? Which bloggers resonate with you and just "get it" with their writing, to the point where you say, "More people need to know about this person?"

An example for Jim is a blog called *Wait But Why*. If Jim were to make a case study of it, he'd talk about the blogger Tim Urban's approachable writing style, his humor, and his hysterical stick-figure cartoons.

Jim could then add media by embedding Urban's TED talk, and tie it back to a personal anecdote, because Jim used Urban's speech-writing process to give a best man speech.

Do you see how you can combine praise, analysis, media, and a personal touch to make a blog post unique and authentic?

Some of Jim's readers may *hate* long blog posts or consider Urban's stick-figure designs immature and unprofessional. That's perfectly okay, because it encourages a discussion in his blog comments or on social media.

You don't have to limit your case study to a blog. You can also cover websites, podcasts, Pinterest boards, YouTube channels, Instagram accounts, LinkedIn groups, and Snapchat accounts.

Companies

Another angle to approach a case study is to look at the companies behind the products and services you use.

Fiona Food Blogger, for instance, is a big fan of the Ankarsrum mixer. She could write a post about the company: its history, including the signature mixer that first came out in 1940, what the company does right, and their customer service.

You, too, could write about companies, whether they have survived the test of time or have had to evolve through the years. Write about companies with interesting people and stories behind them, and whose experiences can be a source of wisdom for your readers. A simple purchase of a new pair of jeans, for example, once lead Jim to write an in-depth case study called, "Dear Levi's, I'm back—How an Iconic Brand Lost Its Way, Then Won Back a Customer 10 years Later."

Solutions

If you've discovered a solution to a nagging problem, one that your readers probably wrestle with, too, then you've got another terrific idea for a blog post.

This is what Lexi did when she wrote, "Essential Oils for Frozen Shoulder." She shared the recipe for the massage oil she applied on her shoulder, the heat pack she used, and the shoulder exercises she found on YouTube and followed… which resulted in the shoulder pain being completely gone after three days.

Here's another example: "3 Options for Nasal Irrigation," where Lexi talks about, not one, but three possible solutions to allergic rhinitis, commonly known as hay fever. She gives the pros and cons of each alternative, and concludes by saying which option works best for specific situations.

Aside from being extremely helpful to your readers, this type of post also tends to do well with search engines, because people nowadays turn to the internet first to find the answers to their problems. So when you discover something that works, do share!

Effective solutions as well as people and companies who are doing things right make excellent topics for blog posts.

Recipe for Success

- Make a list of your favorite bloggers, websites, social media profiles, companies, and solutions.
- Pick one, and think of all the reasons you think it's the best.
- Draw lessons or best practices from the case study that your readers can learn from.
- If you're blogging about a solution, explain exactly what you used and how you used it.
- Support your post with photos (before-and-after photos are particularly effective), videos, and links to other resources.

Blog Post Idea 15: Feature the Bad and the Ugly ***

"'Writer's block' is just a fancy way of saying 'I don't feel like doing any work today.'" - Meagan Spooner

For all the frustration worst-case scenarios cause, they make for another type of case study blog post. Just take the opposite of the last section, and focus on a website, product, or company you hate or are frustrated with.

This can actually be even more interesting, particularly if your case study subject is popular, because you'll be going against conventional wisdom. Share your frustrations with a product or service, and how it's somehow successful *despite* the shortcomings, and explain what you would do differently.

That last part—*what you would do differently*—is a key distinction.

You see, anyone can *rant* on the internet. It's kind of fun, and sometimes you just need to vent. That's why sites like *TimeWarnerCableProblems.com* have existed for more than *seven years running*. But those who post on the site are just complainers.

Some people ruthlessly *attack* individual bloggers, entrepreneurs, or business owners. They're just haters.

You, on the other hand, can vent with maturity,

civility, and understanding—a way that ultimately serves your readers. Here's how:

Step 1: Sure, start with your angry rant or frustration.

Step 2: Then, talk about *why* it makes you so angry.

Step 3: Next, offer a solution to the problem.

Bonus: Step back and look at the bigger picture.

Here are two examples:

In "Efficiency vs. Impatience–A New Yorker Rant," Jim rants about visiting the food trucks in Portland, Oregon during lunch hour, and having to wait in a line 50 people deep for 30 minutes or more for a simple sandwich. The inefficiency made him angry, but there was more to it than that.

Seeing the long line, the last 10 or 20 people are just going to give up and go somewhere else. The food truck is losing money and disappointing customers. And this was happening every single day!

Jim tied this back to his audience, pointing out research that the same thing happens on the web: "For every second a person has to wait for a page to load on a website, the conversion potential drops 7 percent."

Now let's see how Danny rants. In "Serious @PayPal Problems + Open Letter to @DavidMarcus," he gives a blow-by-blow account of doing a product launch and getting the dreaded email from PayPal with the subject line, "We noticed an issue with your account."

What follows is a series of dead ends and U-turns, with Danny leaving seven voicemails in seven days, a fax of several documents, and tweets to David Marcus, then president of PayPal.... only to have nobody return his messages, receive a reminder email about the issue, and get vague email replies from @AskPayPal.

The full account was complete with screenshots, excerpts of the back-and-forth emails, and embedded tweets with Marcus.

Danny didn't publish this post merely to rant. He used his blog, which he refers to as his "megaphone," to speak on behalf of small business owners who suffer through PayPal's vague and intimidating restrictions. He also wrote the post to bring the problem to Marcus's attention, since people who lead large companies are usually unaware of the real problems their customers encounter.

Danny ends the post with a question to Marcus, which any business owner should be asking themselves: "Do you really want to be a business whose customers only stay when they have no other choice?"

With a rant post, you not only get something off your chest. You also spark a discussion. Sometimes your rant can even bring about positive change.

In 2009, a user interface designer named Dustin Curtis was frustrated with the user interface of American Airlines' website. Not only did he complain about it on his blog, but he also proposed a redesigned home page for *AA.com*.

At first, all Curtis got was a generic tweet from the airline. Then, a UX designer and developer from American Airlines wrote Curtis a detailed letter saying why he agreed with him, but why it was so hard to get redesigns like that done due to the massive infrastructure underneath the site, as well as the politics and number of departments that would have to weigh in on such a change.

This went on to spark a larger conversation in the design community, as well as on sites such as *Fast Company*. It took awhile, but the American Airlines site was eventually refreshed.

When you're frustrated with a product or service, it just might be an opportunity for a great blog post.

Recipe for Success

- Think of a product, service, or company that disappoints or frustrates you.
- Write down all the ways you find the subject of your rant frustrating.

- Propose solutions to create the change you want to see.

Blog Post Idea 16: Make Predictions **

"Creativity takes courage." - Henri Matisse

Want to know what the next big tech company is going to be? The one that's going to change the world and take off like a rocket in the stock market?

We do, too. We'd *all* love to know what the next big life-changing hit is going to be, and so do your readers. *Everyone* wants to see the future.

And while you don't have a crystal ball, it sure is fun to make predictions.

- Fiona Food Blogger may wonder: are more and more people going to switch to a plant-based diet?
- For Danny, the question may be: will the top-heavy and expensive college education system collapse by 2020 and be replaced by online education?
- Tommy Tech Blogger may be asking: is the electric car trend over-hyped and will people

hang on to their gas-powered vehicles for decades?

Go ahead, go out on a limb. Write a prediction post, and have fun.

Just remember that you can't pull your predictions out of thin air. Your guess needs to be an *educated* one. And that's possible only when you do your research, when you keep your ear to the ground, stay abreast of what's happening in your niche, and keep track of the comings and goings.

The point isn't to always make the correct predictions. The point is to be able to justify them.

So when you write your prediction post, state your case, and then back it up.

For example, amidst conjectures on the death of guest blogging and other forms of content marketing, Danny responded with the post, "Audience Building in 2016 and Beyond." He went against the popular wisdom about audience building and content marketing. Now, Danny has enough industry knowledge and experience to make his own fearless forecasts, and yet he supported his points with examples, simple logic ("the problem isn't that audience building doesn't work; it's that you've been going about it the wrong way"), and practical advice.

When Jim hit the 250-post milestone, he put out an epic post called, "State of the Industry—Predictions, Rants, Analysis, and Advice for the New Media Entrepreneur." His predictions covered a comprehensive array of media and infotech, including TV sitcoms, movies, Microsoft, smartphone apps, magazines, laptops, electric cars, and online learning, just like Mirasee's Udemy courses.

You don't have to be an industry veteran like Danny or Jim to put your thoughts out there. Even if you're just starting a blog today, a great *first* post might be to list out your predictions and what you believe in, to set the tone for what you'll be covering in the months and years to come.

Or take stock of what happened in the past, and use that as an indicator for where the future is going. That's what Lexi did in the post, "Marketing Lessons of 2013." She wrote about the rise of good content, visuals, and online video in the previous year, and predicted they would get only more popular among online marketers in the future. She also provided lessons so her readers could take action right away.

And unless you're a highly-paid correspondent with millions of people watching your predictions, don't take yourself too seriously. After all, some of your predictions will completely miss the mark. Like the time in 2010 when Jim predicted the fall of Facebook… only to discover in 2015 that the company had made *$18 billion dollars.*

But here's the cool thing. Down the line when you need another idea for a post, you can go back and see how your predictions played out—especially if you were right.

For example, Jim once wrote a post called "7 Reasons Why *The Social Network* Facebook Movie will Be a Huge Success." He explained how he came to that opinion, drawing on research from the writer and director, and poking fun at Justin Timberlake's perm.

Lo and behold, three months later, the box office numbers added up to a tidy $225 million dollars in worldwide gross revenue; Jim was right. He had redeemed himself.

For Jim, it was nice to have a blog post to refer to and brag about months later. He also used that post as an opportunity to tackle a related topic that was a central theme in the movie: the struggle between focusing on the product vs. focusing on the money early on in a startup.

Prediction posts can be fun and educational to write. Whether you end up being right or wrong, it's always interesting to challenge yourself to analyze your niche and come up with your own bold predictions.

Recipe for Success

- Stay informed of the latest developments in your niche.
- Take what you've learned from others and your experience to make your own predictions.
- Support your predictions with examples, logic, and data.

Blog Post Idea 17: Be A Critic ***

"Time heals all wounds; some broken hearts—and most cases of writer's block." - Quentin R. Bufogle

Hold onto your hat, dear reader, because for idea #17, you're getting a two-for-one deal. Here are two ways you can use reviews for blog post ideas.

1) Write a product review

Do you completely adore a product or service?

For Fiona Food Blogger, it could be a chef's knife that feels like an extension of her hand and slices through any food with ease. For Tommy Tech Blogger, it could be the latest smartwatch loaded with whiz-bang functions that makes his life 10 times easier.

It's ok to have a love fest on your blog once in awhile.

Similar to what we covered in Idea #14, writing about best-case scenarios, if you use and like a product, one you're happy to endorse, then write a product review. You'll get traffic from people who are researching the product, and if you do affiliate marketing, reviewing products is a good way to promote products while being honest and useful to your readers.

No need to get overly creative, simply explain what you like about it, and why. Then write what you don't like about it, and why—after all, no product or service is perfect. Your readers will appreciate your candor. You can kick it up a notch by contacting the company, telling them how much you love their product, and asking if they'll donate one you can raffle off to your blog commenters.

In her book review, "First Impressions: *Launch* by Michael Stelzner," Lexi summarizes each chapter and gives her take on it. Instead of spoiling the book for her readers, Lexi's summaries arouse curiosity about the book. Lexi is both generous with her praise ("This [tip] comes in handy for my webinars, where I'm constantly in need of exciting experts to interview.") and candid with her criticism ("I find the rocket ship analogy, shall we say, overly testosterone-y. It would totally resonate with my husband but simply whooshes over my head.")

At the end of the post, she announces a book giveaway. To qualify, readers must post a comment answering the question, "What is your biggest business challenge?" The giveaway not only engages Lexi's readers. It also helps her understand them better—which gives her even more blog post ideas.

In a review of a product, "3 Reasons to Love Buffer for Business (And 3 Reasons Not To)," Lexi gives a balanced critique of Buffer app's business subscription. She incorporates feedback posted on Buffer's blog and clarifies who would get the most benefit from the service. The bottom line is, she writes the review to help her readers decide whether Buffer for Business would make a good investment for them.

As a tech geek, Jim loves to write about gadgets. He could go on and on about his favorite laptops, televisions, microphones, cameras, and headphones. In fact, he once wrote an article called "Best Earbud Headphones for the iPhone," and it stayed in the top 5 ranking on Google for *three years*.

But you don't have to write about the latest products to have a popular review. Whether you're writing about the best blender for smoothies, toys for kids, or apps for social media, think about the best products in your niche. Write from the heart and show your readers why they should care.

2) Link back to and review previous articles

Here's a different kind of review you could do if you've been blogging for a while and have published numerous posts: revisit the oldies but goodies on your blog.

Go through your archives, and make a list of favorite posts that newer readers probably haven't read. These could be the posts you're most proud of, or the ones that have gotten the most traffic (check your Google Analytics to find out). Either way, go back and update them with:

- New or updated information
- Fresh examples and case studies
- Rich media such as videos, images, and embedded tweets
- Insights you've gained since you wrote the post

You could also deconstruct the post, and explain what you were thinking when you wrote the post, what worked, and what didn't.

As an example, Jim shared the milestone of 100 episodes on his blog and podcast with a post, "10 Lessons Learned From 100 Podcast Episodes." Two years was the perfect time to sit back and review what he had learned.

Reviewing a product or service and refreshing an

older post are two of the easiest ways to create a good blog post. It's definitely a tip for your most desperate blogging moments.

Recipe for Success

- Begin your review with an overview of the product or service.
- Be honest about what you like and don't like about the product.
- Share what your readers need to know to make an informed decision about the product.
- Support your assertions with rich media.
- Put new life in new blog posts by refreshing them with new data, examples, and rich media.

Blog Post Idea 18: Show Them How ***

"Tell me and I forget, teach me and I may remember, involve me and I learn." - Ben Franklin

This advice isn't just for teachers and parents. Bloggers would also do well to heed it.

Readers come to your blog to learn something, so one way to get engagement and social shares is to respond when they ask, "How did you do that?"

It's not enough to give advice, no matter how good. Your blog post should also be actionable.

Don't just tell your readers to do something; *teach* them how to do it.

Let us show you what we mean:

When Danny started building an audience, people kept asking him how he did it. How did he go so quickly from a newbie blogger to a recognized authority in marketing and entrepreneurship who's suddenly all over the place? Danny answers that question in "How to Get Traffic to Your Blog (How I Became the Freddy Krueger of Blogging)." He goes into great detail about how he used guest posting to grow the traffic on his site. It includes the four steps he follows to find blogs to write for, a template for pitching to blog editors, and his process for penetrating micro-networks.

Have you ever wanted to make an infographic but had no idea how to even begin? Jim answers that question in "How to Create a Viral Infographic to Market Your Brand." It doesn't just *tell* readers the benefits of creating an infographic—anyone can do that. Instead, Jim walks people through *how* he created one, from sketching it out on paper with a designer, through several iterations, and down to the final product. But then he takes it one step further. He shows the *outcome* of the process: his infographic was picked up by *Lifehacker* and spiked his traffic from 50 visitors to 5,500 visitors, an increase of 10,900%!

Now here's an example for you health buffs. Have you ever wondered, "How can I make it easy to drink a green smoothie everyday?" Lexi's answer is in her post, "Green Smoothies Without Recipes—An Easier Way to Get Healthy." She describes her solution, which is to have a master recipe that's flexible enough to accommodate what most people have in their refrigerators. Then she shares two variations of that recipe, and describes her process for making green smoothies, such as which ingredient to put in the blender first, and why. You'd think making a smoothie was as simple as chucking things in a blender and pushing the on button, right? You'd be surprised.

What would it look like for Tommy Tech Blogger and Fiona Food Blogger to use this idea? Tommy could teach his process for backing up all the data in his computers, tablets, and smartphones. Fiona could teach her system for saving on grocery bills without using coupons.

The possibilities are endless. Just don't fall into the trap of thinking everything you know is common sense, or that everyone else already knows what you know. There are always readers who could learn something from you. Write for them.

Ben Franklin tells us to *involve* people, so they learn. In each of the blog topic ideas we talked about, from case studies and predictions to reviews and how-to articles, there are different ways to actively involve your readers. You could ask them about their own most loved or hated products, contribute to the comments, or enter a contest. Ask them to share their experiences after they've tried what you're teaching.

The other way to help your readers learn is by unselfishly over-delivering on the quality and helpfulness of your post. Spill your secrets! Share the magic beans!

Your reward will be great.

When Jim was researching the best way to run a core conversation at the annual South by Southwest conference (SXSW), he found very little information out there. But he knew people would have questions about the format, so he shared everything he had learned in a blog post.

Even though it wasn't going to benefit him because he'd already delivered his talk, he knew it would help others down the line. It wasn't a disservice to his blog, either. More than three years after he published the post, when someone searches "how to facilitate a core conversation," his post still comes up first.

Make Ben Franklin proud, involve your readers, and

be a great teacher.

Recipe for Success

- Think of a how-to question people often ask you.
- Break down the components of your answer: identify the parts, steps, and elements involved.
- Use photos, screenshots, video, and examples to help your readers carry out the process themselves.

CHAPTER FIVE
Dig Into Life Experiences

By now, you should be well on your way to generating a good number of blog post ideas.

But remember, people aren't just reading your blog because of facts and figures. They also want to know *you*, the person behind the blog.

They want to read about your successes, your failures, and what you've learned along the way. So don't be afraid to bare your soul a little and be vulnerable.

Blog Post Idea 19: Share Your Success ***

"The chief enemy of creativity is good sense." - Pablo Picasso

Think about a time when something went right for you. Whether it was a business deal, a consulting session, or a product launch, reflect on an occasion when you had a plan, put in the time, and all your hard work paid off.

Then, write a post explaining how it all happened. You're not doing this to brag. You're doing this to draw out the lessons you learned from the experience— lessons your readers can learn from as well.

Fiona Food Blogger, for example, could write a post about how she pulled off a dinner party for 30 people without hiring a caterer and without going insane— and her friends still talk about it years later. And for his tech blog, Tommy could write a post about how he got technical support for a problem with his laptop, even when the warranty had run out.

In "How a Tiny Blog Landed Guy Kawasaki (and *Copyblogger*!)," Danny blogs about how he, a newbie in the online space at the time, connected with Jon Morrow of Copyblogger, got an interview with Guy Kawasaki, and landed a post on ProBlogger. He concluded the post with nine lessons for bloggers.

A similar post was "How I Created, Planned, and Got Sponsorship for a Successful Conference in Less than 60 Days." In more than 1,300 words, Jim shares the details of a conference he and a friend launched from scratch, including what they did to make it a success.

Your success post doesn't have to be about a dramatic life-changer, just as long as it's something your readers aspire for as well. For example, in "7 Ways to Find Freelancing Work: What's Working Now," Lexi talks about how she found freelancing work after two years of being employed full-time and completely neglecting her freelance writing practice.

So if you've had some success in your blog niche, before you rush off for the next exciting thing, take a moment to relish it—and share insights with your readers.

Recipe for Success

- Reflect on something that went well for you.
- Analyze what worked and what went wrong.
- Draw lessons and insights your readers can benefit from.

Blog Post Idea 20: Turn Failures Into Posts ***

"Failure is so important. We speak about success all the time. It is the ability to resist failure or use failure that

often leads to greater success. I've met people who don't want to try for fear of failing." - J.K. Rowling

If there's anything people love reading about more than a great success, it's an epic failure.

Failure stories make us feel better about ourselves: "Glad I'm not the only messed-up person around here."

And they can inspire us to overcome failure and achieve success: "If that idiot survived a disaster that big, then so can I!"

A post about your most challenging experiences is likely to be powerful by virtue of how intense the original experience was for you, and you don't have to make up anything original or creative—just tell it like it is (or, *was*), and explain what you learned from the process.

Danny knows this first-hand. He bravely tells the story of the demise of his first business, an educational software company, that crumbled under the weight of the recession and left him more than a quarter of a million dollars in debt, in "Business Failure or Strategic Relocation?: It's Your Call." It's one of his most successful guest posts.

And while Danny delved into the tough times at one single company, Jim once explored "What Six Crappy Part-time Jobs Taught Me About Life." Long before

Jim was fortunate enough to land jobs at great companies like ESPN, WIRED, and Mirasee, he was a paperboy, dishwasher, warehouse worker, and janitor at a bar. Not quite so glamorous, right?

In "Update on My Income Challenge," Lexi admits failing to achieve a goal she publicly declared on her blog. "It's embarrassing to admit I've failed, but I have," she writes. She then explains why she failed, but she doesn't end there. She shares what she plans to do to get back on track. Judging from the comments, her readers appreciated Lexi's transparency in this post.

The key to a good failure post is not to dwell on the failure itself, but to analyze what happened and why, what you learned, and what you would do differently... so your readers can learn from your mistakes.

Going back to our bloggers, Tommy Tech Blogger's failure post could be about how he tried to fix the screen of his smartphone by himself... only to cause more damage and incur higher costs to get it fixed properly.

And Fiona Food Blogger could write about her numerous failed attempts to bake the softest, fluffiest, 100% whole wheat bread.

You can't avoid failure, but you *can* turn it into a blog post.

Recipe for Success

- Think of a time when things didn't go as planned, you didn't get the results you hoped for, and you failed.
- Analyze what happened: What went wrong? Why did you fail?
- Share the lessons you learned from the failure and what you would do differently if you could do it all over again.

Blog Post Idea 21: Tell Your Story ***

"Creativity has got to start with humanity and when you're a human being, you feel, you suffer. You're gay, you're sick, you're nervous or whatever." - Marilyn Monroe

If you haven't figured it out yet, your blog is not just about business, but also about the connection your reader has with you. So the final blog post idea we have for you is to tell your story.

If you're ready to kick things into overdrive, write a post about a powerful and deeply personal experience.

For this, you've got to dig deep, and pull up a formative story in your life—such as a crisis you overcame—and how you became a better and happier person for it.

It's not easy to bare your soul. You'll feel naked and vulnerable. You'll make yourself a target for judgment.

On the other hand, in terms of creating content, it's easy in the sense that you're writing about something that already happened to you.

For example, as a weekend warrior and lifelong athlete, Jim thought he was invincible. That was, until he had a nasty mountain bike accident and shattered his arm. The experience gave him a fresh perspective about social media and relationships, which he writes about in "Why a Distal Humerus Fracture has NOTHING to Do with Social Media."

A year later, he realized how ludicrous it was to gripe about his broken arm, when a friend and former co-worker passed. The result was another reflective post, "8 Life Lessons from a Fallen Friend." How's that for gaining perspective?

Other powerful examples include Danny Brown's post on his failed suicide attempt, "You Don't Have to Die to Live," Jon Morrow's account of his childhood fight for survival in "On Dying, Mothers, and Fighting for Your Ideas," Brian Clark's telling of a life-threatening experience in "The Snowboard, the Subdural Hematoma, and the Secret of Life."

Sometimes it's not a specific event but an intense feeling that can drive a personal post, such as Lexi's "A

Ghost Writer's Dilemma." She bares her frustration at ghostwriting great stuff... only to see her clients get all the credit. No surprise, this post got a lot of comments from her readers, many of whom are freelance writers themselves.

The point is not to depress yourself or your readers, but to inspire you to dig deeper for those stories that will resonate, the stories about life itself.

In fact, your stories can be happy ones, such as when Danny blogged about his Hindu-Jewish wedding ("Our Magical Hin-Jew Wedding") and the emotional roller coaster of dealing with infertility and finally having a baby ("Anxiety, Surrender, and the Magical Beauty of Things Happening at the Right Time"). The posts make Danny's readers feel like they're part of his family, since they become privy to the details of his courtship, wedding, and journey into parenthood.

Sometimes you can relate these life stories with lessons for your readers. But other times, you simply want to share an experience or insight. Either way, remember, if you can't write something useful, you must at least be entertaining.

Recipe for Success

- Look into your life experiences for the most intense events that can elicit a strong emotional response from your readers.
- Use elements to make your post entertaining, whether it's drama, tragedy, or comedy.
- If possible, make the post relevant to your readers by pointing out what they can learn from your experience.

CONCLUSION
Your Next Steps

"Writing is thinking on paper, or talking to someone on paper. If you can think clearly, or if you can talk to someone about the things you know and care about, you can write—with confidence and enjoyment." - William Zinsser

If we've done our job, you started reading this book struggling to come up with blog post ideas, and are finishing it with enough creative inspiration not only for your next few posts, but to keep you going for months on end.

Becoming a successful blogger is less about the notebook you choose or the program you write with, and more about being receptive to the world around you and translating your ideas into words.

Lexi likes to say, "First live, then blog."

If you live and breathe your niche, you'll never run out of ideas for your blog. So immerse yourself in your niche. Go out and see the world. Read relevant blogs, books, and magazines, attend live events, and meet interesting people. That way, you'll always have fodder for content. Learn. Explore. Discover every angle, aspect, and nuance of your niche.

Then become a storyteller. Blog about your experiences and your thoughts. What are you curious about? What made you sit up and take notice? Who did you meet?

We've given you the tools you need to kiss writer's block goodbye and keep blogging. The rest is up to you. As long as you know and care about something, you'll always have something to blog about.

You've finished the book. Now get blogging!

Blog Post Ideas Extras

Free PDF Cheat Sheet + Blogging Expert Interviews + Online Video Companion Course

Get a one-page summary of the 21 blog post ideas, access to interviews of blogging experts, and a discounted price to the companion course!

Free PDF Cheat Sheet
Always have 21 blog post ideas within easy reach with this colorful cheat sheet.

Blogging Expert Interviews
Successful bloggers reveal how they bust through writer's block.

Online Video Companion Course – 50% off coupon
Enrich your discovery of the blog post ideas in this book. The video-based companion course is a different experience.

- 60+ minutes of video instructions
- Entertaining and educational

- Video walk-throughs of sample posts
- Bonus interviews of bloggers who've become published authors

Get your free cheat sheet, bonus interviews, and course coupon:

http://mrse.co/blog-ideas-extras

About Danny Iny

Danny Iny (@DannyIny) is the founder of Mirasee, host of the Business Reimagined podcast, best-selling author of multiple books including *Engagement from Scratch!*, *The Audience Revolution*, and *Teach and Grow Rich*, and creator of the acclaimed *Audience Business Masterclass* and *Course Builder's Laboratory* training programs, which have together graduated over 4,000 value-driven online entrepreneurs. He lives in Montreal, Canada with his wonderful wife (and business partner) Bhoomi, and their beautiful baby daughter.

Also by Danny Iny:

- Teach and Grow Rich: The Emerging Opportunity for Global Impact, Freedom, and Wealth

- The Audience Revolution: The Smarter Way to Build a Business, Make a Difference, and Change the World

- Engagement from Scratch!: How Super-Community Builders Create a Loyal Audience and How You Can Do the Same!

About Jim Hopkinson

Jim Hopkinson (@HopkinsonReport) is a digital media professional helping to reimagine education and training for the new economy. As Director of Courses at Mirasee, he helps entrepreneurs get the training they need to put their ideas into the world by building and scaling a profitable online business. He is also the author of *Salary Tutor*, and helps ambitious professionals negotiate higher salaries. He lives in New York City, is an avid sports fan and tech geek, and enjoys mentoring young business professionals.

Also by Jim Hopkinson:

- Salary Tutor: Learn the Salary Negotiation Secrets No One Ever Taught You

About Alexis Rodrigo

Alexis "Lexi" Rodrigo (@LexiRodrigo) is a copywriter who creates content to build authority, strengthen community, and inspire action. Before becoming growth writer at **Mirasee**, she juggled blogs in diverse industries, from eco-friendly living to public relations, from freelancing to digital marketing. She has been a ghostwriter for several CEOs, created information products, and authored *The Savvy Freelancer's Website Secrets*. She also has extensive experience in communication and fundraising for nonprofits. She lives in Windsor, Canada, with her husband and three children.

Also by Lexi Rodrigo:

- *The Savvy Freelancer's Website Secrets: How to Create a Client Magnet Online*

- *Video Marketing for the Clueless*

- *Don't Get Sick for Beauty's Sake! 12 Toxic Ingredients in Cosmetics & Beauty Products*

Acknowledgments

This book is the product of many years of blogging. It wouldn't have been possible without our mentors and teachers:

From Danny: To Jon Morrow, who first showed me the power that writing and blogging has to move people's hearts and minds, and build a business based on ideas that resonate and matter. Thank you, Jon.

From Jim: To my boss Jim McGee when I was at ESPN, who gave our group the freedom to write creatively. To Dan Shar when I was at WIRED, who told me, "I don't know what all your writing is going to lead to, but keep doing it." And to my friend Bobby Shanes, my travel partner in crime who showed me a larger world beyond sports and technology.

From Lexi: To Offie Valdecanas, for teaching me that the most important part of any writing is the reader. To Dr. Nicholas Alipui, former UNICEF Representative in the Philippines, for allowing me to blog about our breastfeeding advocacy—before we even understood blogs. To Alice Seba, Kelly McCausey, and Nicole Dean, for getting me started online. And to Jon Morrow, for challenging me to go from good to great.

Thank you for showing us all the doors blogging opens.

We could never demonstrate enough how much we appreciate the readers we discovered behind those doors, who gave us their most valuable gifts: their time and attention.

We also thank our Mirasee family for cheering us on, making us laugh even when deadlines are tight, and creating a joyful environment to work in.

And to our families. Thank you for being the wind beneath our wings.

Printed in Great Britain
by Amazon